Christmas
ABC

Christmas
ABC

Adapted from a poem by Carolyn Wells (1862–1942)

THE METROPOLITAN MUSEUM OF ART

HARRY N. ABRAMS, INC., PUBLISHERS

A is
for Angel
who graces
the tree.

B is for
Bells that
chime out
in glee.

 is
for Candle
to light
Christmas Eve.

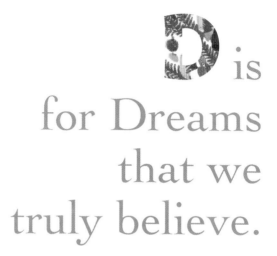 is
for Dreams
that we
truly believe.

C·KRENEK

E is for
Evergreens
cut for
the room.

F is for
Flowers of
exquisite
perfume.

G is for
Gifts that
bring us
delight.

H is for Holly with red berries bright.

I is
for Ice,
so shining
and clear.

J is
for Joy
at this time
of year.

K is for Kings who came a long way.

L is for
Lights that
brighten
the day.

 is
for Mother,
who's trimming
the bough.

N is for Night, see the stars sparkling now.

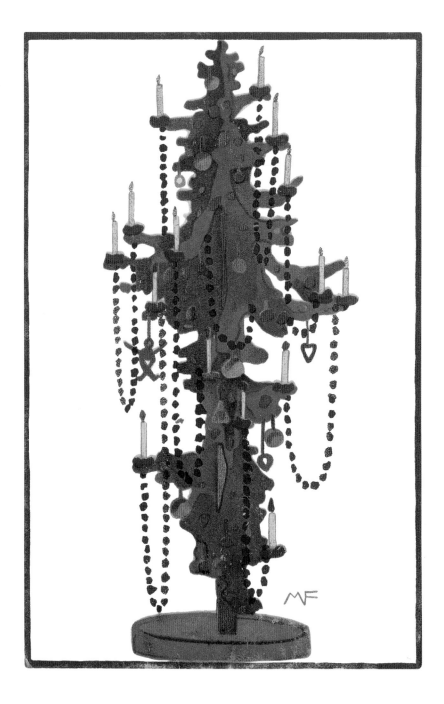

O is for
Ornaments,
dazzling
with light.

P is
for Parties
with friends
Christmas
night.

 is
Quadrille, a
dance we
will do.

R is for Ribbons, bright red, green, and blue.

S is for Snow that falls silently down.

T is for Toys that old Santa brings 'round.

U is for
Uproar
that goes
on all day.

V is for
Voices that
sing out
and pray.

W is for
Wreaths to
be hung in
the hall.

X is for Xmas, with pleasures for all.

Y is for Yuletide, and may yours be bright.

Z is for
Zest shown
from morning
till night.

The illustrations reproduced in this book are from color lithographic postcards
designed by artists at the Wiener Werkstätte, in Vienna, Austria, between late 1907 and 1914.
All of the works of art are from the Department of Drawings and Prints
of The Metropolitan Museum of Art.

Published in 2002 by The Metropolitan Museum of Art, New York,
and Harry N. Abrams, Incorporated, New York.
Copyright © 2002 by The Metropolitan Museum of Art

First Edition
Printed in Hong Kong
11 10 09 08 07 06 05 04 03   5 4 3 2

Produced by the Department of Special Publications, The Metropolitan Museum of Art:
Robie Rogge, Publishing Manager; Judith Cressy, Project Editor; Anna Raff, Designer.
All photography by The Metropolitan Museum of Art Photograph Studio.

Visit the Museum's Web site: www.metmuseum.org

Library of Congress Cataloging-in-Publication Data

Wells, Carolyn, d. 1942.
  Christmas ABC / adapted from a poem by Carolyn Wells.
     p. cm.
Summary: A poem in which every letter of the alphabet describes
a different aspect of Christmas and its celebration.
  ISBN 1-58839-054-3 (MMA).—ISBN 0-8109-3496-5 (Abrams)
  1. Christmas—Juvenile poetry. 2. Children's poetry, American. 3.
Alphabet rhymes. [1. Christmas—Poetry. 2. American poetry. 3.
Alphabet.] I. Wells, Carolyn, d. 1942. Christmas alphabet. II. Title.
  PS3545.E533 C44 2002
  811' .52[E]—dc21
                                                        2002002631

Harry N. Abrams
100 Fifth Avenue
New York, NY 10011
www.abramsbooks.com

Abrams is a subsidiary of

LA MARTINIÈRE
G R O U P E